RUBANK EDUCATIONAL LIBRARY No. 92

RUBANK

Advanced Method

O B O E
VOL. I

H. VOXMAN
AND
WM. GOWER

AN OUTLINED COURSE OF STUDY
DESIGNED TO FOLLOW UP ANY
OF THE VARIOUS ELEMENTARY
AND INTERMEDIATE METHODS

RUBANK®

HAL•LEONARD®
CORPORATION
7777 W. BLUEMOUND RD. P.O. BOX 13819 MILWAUKEE, WI 53213

NOTE

THE RUBANK ADVANCED METHOD for Oboe is published in two volumes, the course of study being divided in the following manner:

Vol. I { Keys of C, F, G, Bb, and D Major.
{ Keys of A, D, E, G, and B Minor.

Vol. II { Keys of Eb, A, Ab, E, Db, and B Major.
{ Keys of C, F#, F, and C# Minor.

PREFACE

THIS METHOD is designed to follow any of the various Elementary and Intermediate instruction series, or Elementary instruction series comprising two or more volumes, depending upon the previous development of the student. The authors have found it necessary in their teaching experience to draw from many sources in order to provide a progressive course of study. The present publication assembles in two volumes, the material essential to a well-rounded musical development.

THE OUTLINES, one of which is included in each of the respective volumes, tend to afford an objective picture of the student's progress. They will facilitate the ranking of members in a large ensemble or they may serve as a basis for awards of merit. In addition, a one-sided development along strictly technical or strictly melodic lines is avoided. The use of these outlines, however, is not imperative and they may be discarded at the discretion of the teacher.

H. Voxman — Wm. Gower

OUTLINE
OF
RUBANK ADVANCED METHOD
FOR
OBOE, Vol. I
BY
H. Voxman and Wm. Gower

UNIT	SCALES and ARPEGGIOS	(Key)	MELODIC INTERPRETATION	ARTICULATION	FINGER EXERCISES	ORNAMENTS	SOLOS	UNIT COMPLETED
1	5 (1) 6 (5)	C	19 (1)	44 (1)	54 [1-2]	60 (1)	66 (1)	
2	5 (2) 6 (6)	C	20 (2)	44 (2)	54 [3-4]	60 (1)	66 (1)	
3	5 (3) 6 (7)	C	21 (3)	45 (3)	54 [5-7]	60 (2)	66 (1)	
4	6 (4) (8)	C	22 (4)	45 (4)	54 [8-12]	60 (3)	66 (1)	
5	6 (9)	a	23 (5)	45 (5)	54 [13-14]	60 (4)	66 (1)	
6	6 (10) 7 (12)	a	24 (6)	46 (6)	54 [15-16]	60 (5)	66 (1)	
7	7 (11) (13)	a	25 (7)	46 (6)	54 [17-20]	61 (6)	66 (2)	
8	7 (14) (15)	a	25 (7)	46 (7)	54 [21-24]	61 (7)	66 (2)	
9	7 (16) (17) 9 (21)	F	26 (8)	47 (8)	54 [25-30]	61 (8)	66 (2)	
10	8 (18) 9 (22)	F	26 (9)	47 (9)	54 [31-36]	61 (9)	66 (2)	
11	8 (19) 9 (23)	F	28 (10)	47 (10)	55 [37-40]	61 (10)	66 (2)	
12	8 (20) 9 (24)	F	28 (10)	47 (10)	55 [41-44]	62 (11)	66 (2)	
13	9 (25)	d	29 (11)	47 (11)	55 [45-52]	62 (11)	67 (3)	
14	9 (26)	d	30 (12)	48 (12)	55 [53-56]	62 (12)	67 (3)	
15	9 (27) 10 (28) (29)	d	30 (12)	48 (13)	55 [57-60]	62 (13)	67 (3)	
16	10 (30) 11 (35) (36)	G	31 (13)	48 (14)	55 [61-64]	62 (14)	67 (3)	
17	10 (31) 11 (37)	G	31 (13)	49 (15)	55 [65-68]	62 (15)	67 (3)	
18	10 (32) 11 (38)	G	32 (14)	49 (16)	56 [69-72]	62 (16)	67 (3)	
19	11 (33) (34)	G	32 (14)	49 (16)	56 [73-76]	63 (17)	67 (4)	
20	11 (39)	e	32 (15)	49 (17)	56 [77-80]	63 (18) (19)	67 (4)	
21	12 (40) (42) (43)	e	33 (16)	50 (18)	56 [81-84]	63 (20) (21)	67 (4)	
22	12 (41) (44) (45)	e	33 (16)	50 (18)	56 [85-88]	63 (22)	67 (4)	
23	13 (46) 14 (50)	Bb	34 (17)	50 (19)	56 [89-92]	63 (23)	67 (4)	
24	13 (47) 14 (51)	Bb	35 (18)	50 (19)	56 [93-96]	63 (24)	67 (4)	
25	13 (48) 14 (52)	Bb	35 (19)	50 (20)	56 [97-100]	63 (25)	68 (5)	
26	14 (49) (53)	Bb	35 (19)	50 (20)	56 [101-104]	64 (26)	68 (5)	
27	15 (54)	g	36 (20)	51 (21)	56 [105-108]	64 (27)	68 (5)	
28	15 (55) (58)	g	37 (21)	51 (22)	57 [109-112]	64 (28)	68 (5)	
29	15 (56) (57) (59)	g	37 (21)	51 (22)	57 [113-116]	64 (29)	68 (5)	
30	16 (60) 17 (65)	D	38 (22)	52 (23)	57 [117-120]	65 (30)	68 (5)	
31	16 (61) 17 (66)	D	38 (22)	52 (24)	57 [121-124]	65 (31)	70 (6)	
32	16 (62) 17 (67) (68)	D	40 (23)	52 (25)	57 [125-128]	65 (32)	70 (6)	
33	16 (63) 17 (64)	D	40 (23)	52 (26)	57 [129-132]	65 (33)	70 (6)	
34	18 (69)	b	42 (24)	53 (27)	57 [133-136]	65 (34)	70 (6)	
35	18 (70) (71)	b	42 (25)	53 (28)	57 [137-140]	65 (35)	70 (6)	
36	18 (72) (73) (74)	b	42 (25)	53 (28)	57 [141-144]	65 (35)	70 (6)	

NUMERALS designate page number.
ENCIRCLED NUMBERS designate exercise number.
[5-7] indicates exercises 5, 6 and 7, etc.
COMPLETED EXERCISES may be indicated by crossing out the rings, thus, ⊗.

PRACTICE AND GRADE REPORT

SECOND SEMESTER

Student's Name _____

Date _____

Week	Sun.	Mon.	Tue.	Wed.	Thu.	Fri.	Sat.	Total	Parent's Signature	Grade
1										
2										
3										
4										
5										
6										
7										
8										
9										
10										
11										
12										
13										
14										
15										
16										
17										
18										
19										
20										

Semester Grade _____

Instructor's Signature _____

FIRST SEMESTER

Student's Name _____

Date _____

Week	Sun.	Mon.	Tue.	Wed.	Thu.	Fri.	Sat.	Total	Parent's Signature	Grade
1										
2										
3										
4										
5										
6										
7										
8										
9										
10										
11										
12										
13										
14										
15										
16										
17										
18										
19										
20										

Semester Grade _____

Instructor's Signature _____

Scales and Arpeggios
C Major

Various articulations may be used in the chromatic, the interval, and the chord studies at the instructor's option.

Thirds

Common chord

Diminished 7th chord

F Major

18

19

20

Common chord

Diminished 7th chord

G Major

simile

simile

Thirds

Common chord

Dominant 7th chord

E Minor

Natural **Harmonic**

Melodic

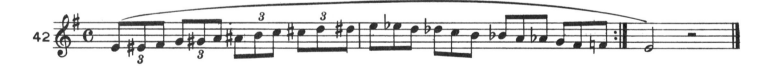

Thirds

Common chord

Diminished 7th chord

Bb Major

NOTE- Oboists not having the low Bb on their instruments may replace that note with its octave in the following exercises. The use of the "forked" F will henceforth be left to the discretion of the student.

Thirds

Common chord

Dominant 7th chord

G Minor

Natural **Harmonic**

54

Melodic

55

56

57

Common chord

58

Diminished 7th chord

59

D Major

64

65

Thirds

66

Common chord

67

Dominant 7th chord

68

B Minor

Studies in Melodic Interpretation
For One or Two Part Playing

The following studies are designed to aid in the development of the student's interpretative ability. Careful attention to the marks of expression is essential to effective use of the material Pencil the technically difficult passages and devote extra time to their mastery.

In rhythmic music in the more rapid tempi (marches, dances, etc.) tones that are equal divisions of the beat are played somewhat detached (staccato). Tones that equal a beat or are multiples of a beat are held full value. Tones followed by rests are usually held full value. This point should be especially observed in slow music.

BROD

Moderato (♩ = 88)

Copyright MCMXL by Rubank, Inc. Chicago, Ill.
International Copyright Secured

MOZART

Tempo di Menuetto

2

TRIO

Menuetto D.C.

Andante grazioso(♪=120)

Moderato (♩=84)

BARRET

4

BARRET

Moderato

5

smorzando

24

Practice No. 6 first in three counts to the measure and then in one.

HOHMANN

Allegretto

VERROUST

BARRET

Allegretto (♩=104)

8

Allegretto

FODOR

9

All° non troppo (♩=76)

10

Larghetto

12

NIEMANN

Allegro

13

NIEMANN

Allegretto

14

NIEMANN

Andantino

15

VERROUST

Andante

16

a tempo

BERR

Moderato

17

NIEMANN

Allegro non tanto

18

HOHMANN

Allegro

19

Moderato (♩ = 88)

BARRET

20

cresc.   dim.

a tempo

poco rit.   p

rf

f

BROD

Andante (♪=152)

21

p

mf   sf   f

CARNAZZO

Allegro moderato

NIEMANN

23

TRIO

Allegro maestoso

NIEMANN

BAERMANN

Allegro vivace

Studies in Articulation

In all exercises where no tempo is indicated, the student should play the study as rapidly as is consistent with tonal control and technical accuracy. The first practice on each exercise should be done very slowly in order that the articulation may be carefully observed.

In allegro tempi figures similar to should be performed etc. The figure should be played

The letter F indicates the use of the "forked" fingering On oboes not having a resonance key it is generally advisable to use the Eb key (number 5 or 5B) in addition.

The material for this section is taken from the works of Barret, Brod, Sellner, Salviani, Niemann, etc.

45

Tempo di Tarantella (in fast two)

simile

simile

48

From this point on the use of the "forked" F is left to the judgment of the student.

Leggiero (♩=88)

15

p   *sempre stacc.*

f

Tempo di Valse (♪=172)

16

f   *p*

f

dim.   *p*   Fine   *f*

D.C. al Fine

17

Allegro con moto

18

19

All.º rustico

20

Brillante

Exercises in Fingering

Practice these exercises slowly and increase in rapidity as the difficulties in fingering are overcome.

Finger F unless otherwise indicated. The Eb key (5 or 5B) should be used with the "forked" F on instruments not having a resonance key.

Practice also for C♯.

Retain A♭ fingering.

56

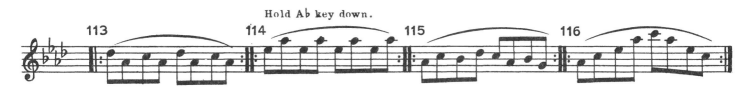

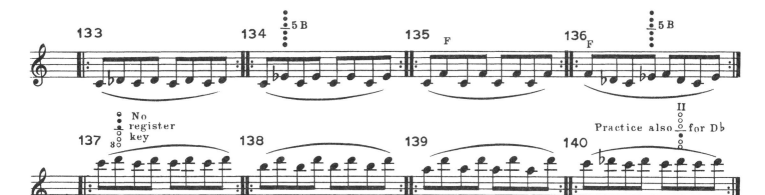

Table of Trills for the Conservatory System Oboe

Use first octave key (I) on trills from ♯𝅝 to ♯𝅝

Use second octave key (II) on trills from ♯𝅝 to ♭𝅝

Above 𝅝 use octave key only when indicated.

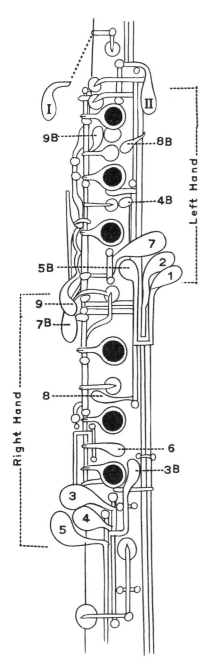

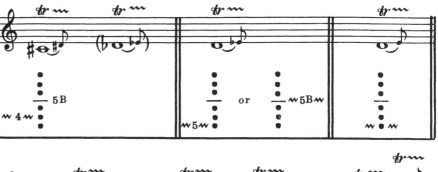

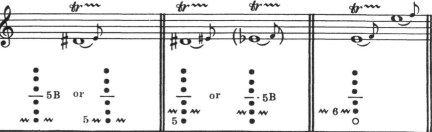

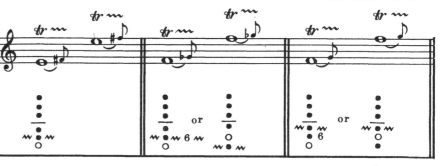

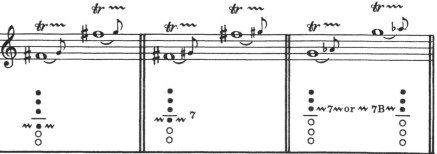

(1) Only practicable on oboes having key 3B.

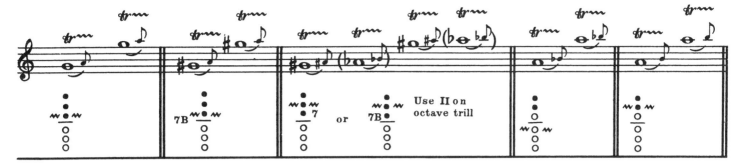

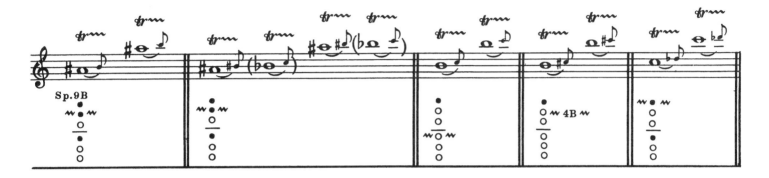

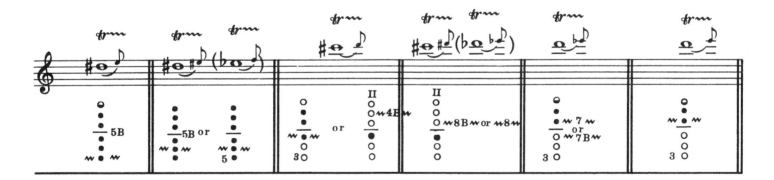

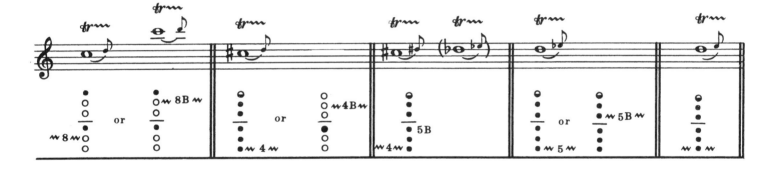

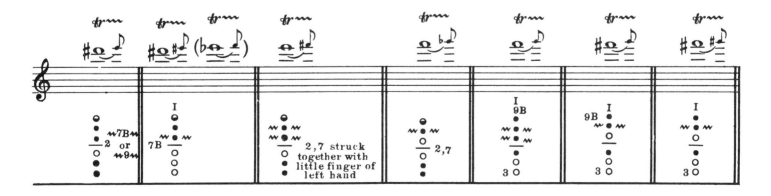

Musical Ornamentation (Embellishments)

The following treatment of ornamentation is by no means complete. It is presented here only as a guide to the execution of those ornaments which the student may encounter at this stage of his musical development. There are different manners of performing the same ornament.

The Trill (Shake)

The <u>trill</u> (or shake) consists of the rapid alternation of two tones. They are represented by the printed note (called the principal note) and the next tone above in the diatonic scale. The interval between the two tones may be either a half-step or a whole-step. The signs for the trill are *tr* and ∿

An accidental when used in conjunction with the trill sign affects the upper note of the trill.

Be sure to look up each trill fingering in the table.

Play as in No. 1

* The asterisks indicate trill fingerings that differ from fundamental fingerings.

Grace Notes (Appoggiatura)

The grace notes are indicated by notes of a smaller size. They may be divided into two classes, long and short.

from "Serenade" Haydn

In instrumental music of recent composition, the short grace notes should occupy as little time as possible and that value is taken preceding the principal note. They may be single, double, triple, or quadruple. The single short grace note is printed as a small eighth note with a stroke through its hook. It is not to be accented. Use trill fingerings when fundamental fingerings are too difficult.

Excerpt from "Rustic Wedding" Goldmark

Excerpt from "Moment Musical" Schubert

Excerpt from "Turkish March" Beethoven

The Mordent

The *short* mordent (᷍) consists of a single rapid alternation of the principal note with its lower auxiliary. Two or more alternations are executed in the *long* mordent.

The *short inverted* mordent (᷍) does not have the cross line. In it the lower auxiliary is replaced by the upper. It is the more commonly used mordent in music for the wind instruments.

The mordent takes its value from the principal note.

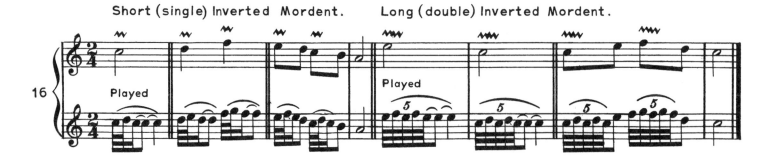

Short (single) Inverted Mordent.　Long (double) Inverted Mordent.

from "Menuet" Schubert

In trills of sufficient length a special ending is generally used whether indicated or not.

The closing of the trill consists of two tones: the scale tone below the principal note and the principal note.

In long trills of a solo character, it is good taste to commence slowly and gradually increase the speed. Practice the following exercises in the manner of both examples 1 and 2.

The Turn (Gruppetto)

The turn consists of four tones: the next scale tone above the principal tone, the principal tone itself, the tone below the principal tone, and the principal tone again.

When the turn (∞) is placed to the right of the note, the principal tone is held almost to its full value, then the turn is played just before the next melody tone. In this case (Ex. 1, 2, 3, 4, and 5) the four tones are of equal length.

When the turn is placed between a dotted note and another note having the same value as the dot (Ex. 6 and 8), the turn is then played with the last note of the turn taking the place of the dot, making two notes of the same value. The turn sign after a dotted note will indicate that one melody note lies hidden in the dot.

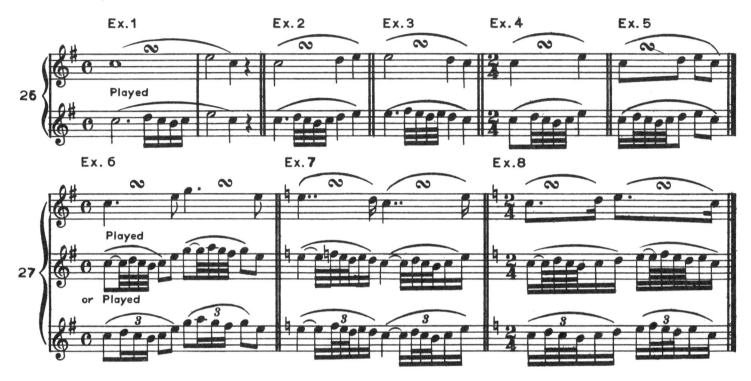

Sometimes an accidental sign occurs with the turn, and in this case, when written above the sign, it refers to the highest tone of the turn, but when written below, to the lowest. (Ex. 2 and 1).

When the turn is placed over a note (Ex. 3) the tones are usually played quickly, and the fourth tone is then held until the time value of the note has expired.

In the inverted turn (Ex. 4) the order of tones is reversed, the lowest one coming first, the principal next, the highest third and the principal tone again, last. The inverted turn is indicated by the ordinary turn sign reversed: ∾ or by ⸙.

ARBAN

ARBAN

30

31

32

33

34

35

SOLOS
Melody

SCHUMANN

Sarabande
from Concerto in G Minor

HANDEL

Aria
from Der Freischütz

C. M. von WEBER

Solvejg's Song

GRIEG

Alleluja
from Exultate Jubilate

MOZART

Allegro non troppo

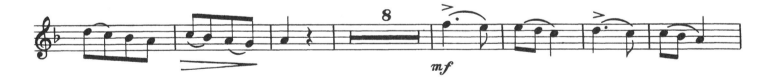

Nocturne

Oboe

L. BASSI

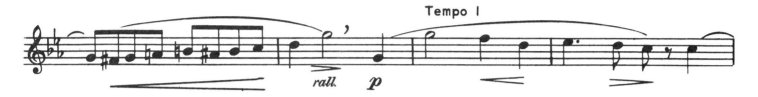